CW00548272

Carolus Linnaeus

THE LIFE AND WORKS OF THE FATHER OF MODERN TAXONOMY

Naming the World Grade 5 | Children's Biographies

DISSECTED LIVES
auto biographies

First Edition, 2020

Published in the United States by Speedy Publishing LLC, 40 E Main Street, Newark, Delaware 19711 USA.

© 2020 Dissected Lives Books, an imprint of Speedy Publishing LLC

Dissected Lives Books are available at special discounts when purchased in bulk for industrial and sales-promotional use. For details contact our Special Sales Team at Speedy Publishing LLC, 40 E Main Street, Newark, Delaware 19711 USA. Telephone (888) 248-4521 Fax: (210) 519-4043.

10 9 8 7 6 * 5 4 3 2 1

Print Edition: 9781541953871
Digital Edition: 9781541956872
Hardcover Edition: 9781541979543

See the world in pictures. Build your knowledge in style.
www.speedypublishing.com

Table of Contents

MILLIONS OF LIVING THINGS MAKE THEIR HOME ON EARTH.

Millions of living things make their home on planet Earth, so it is difficult for scientists to keep them all straight. In fact, a few hundred years ago, it was common for biologists to get confused about certain plants and animals. How is one plant related to another? Is a brown bear the same animal as a black bear, or are they different animals?

To help scientists better understand the relationship between all living things, a Swedish botanist named Carolus Linnaeus took on the daunting[1] task of classifying every living thing on Earth back in the 1700s. Let's see how he hit upon his method of classification that is still being used today.

---

[1] Daunting – Challenging or intimidating

CAROLUS LINNAEUS

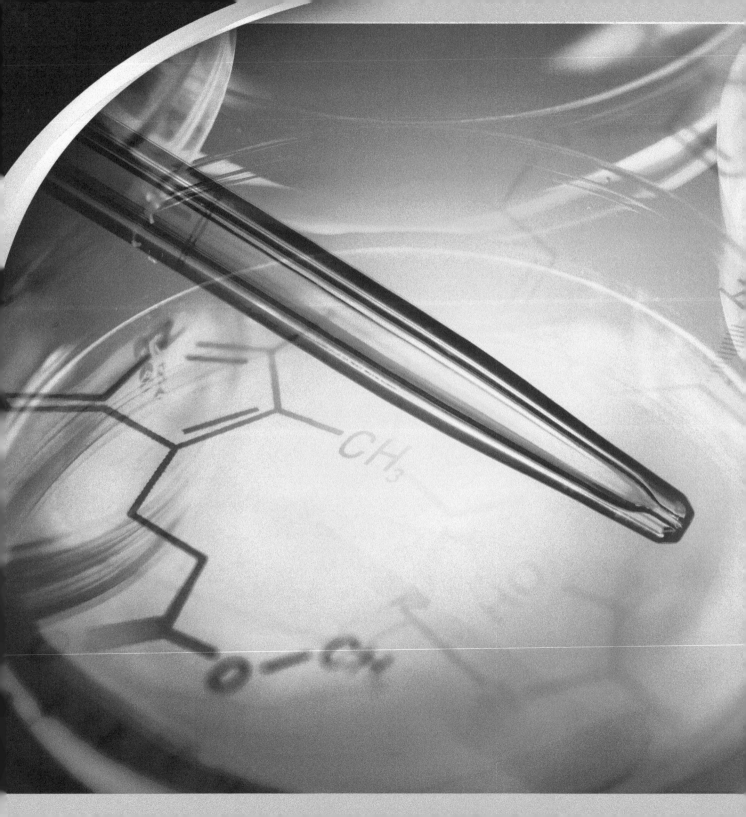

Naming Plants and Animals

If you have ever had to help your family pick out a good name for a new pet, you probably know that it is not as easy of a task as it seems. First, there are so many options to choose from. Plus, you don't want to select a name that is too similar to a family member's name or another pet's name because that will cause confusion. Lastly, all family members have their own opinion on the perfect name so there probably was some debate and disagreement.

A PUPPY HAVING A NAP IN A BASKET WITH HIS NAME SPELLED USING ALPHABET BLOCKS.

Heb. Gamal. *Kameeldier.*

Heb. Bekrach. Dromedarius, *Dromedarij.*

PRE-BINOMIAL CLASSIFICATION OF SPECIES. TWO DIFFERENT SPECIES OF THE GENUS CAMEL ARE NAMED IN HEBREW, LATIN AND DUTCH, ALTHOUGH ONLY ONE SPECIES, THE BACTRIAN IS DEPICTED.

It is the same with naming newly discovered plants and animals. In addition to the issues you encountered, there is the problem of distance and language. A scientist in Germany, for example, may name a plant a Germanic word while a scientist in France may call the exact name plant by a different name...a French-sounding one.

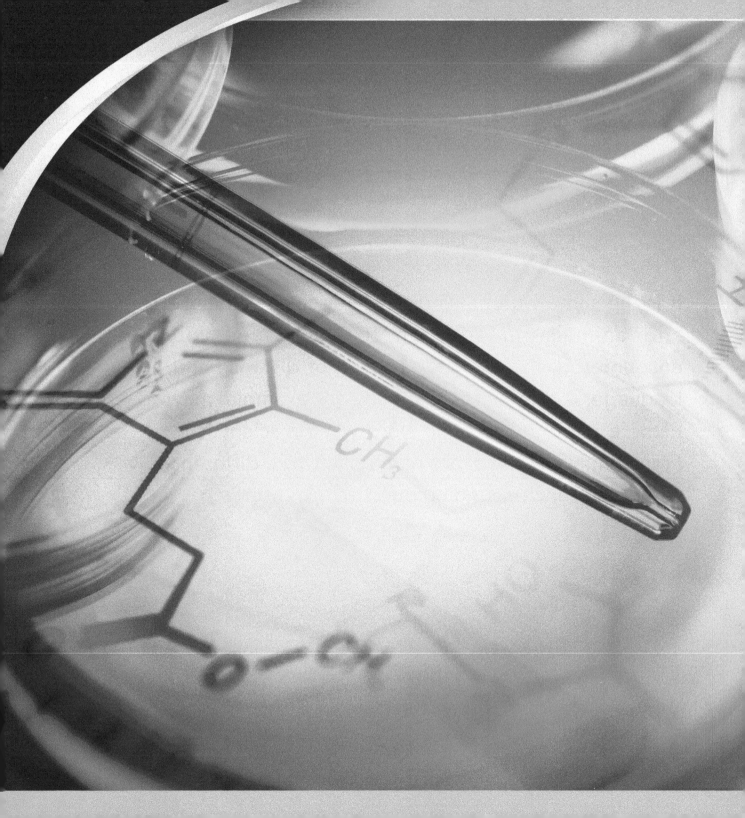

What Does Taxonomy Mean?

The word "taxonomy" means the scientific field that pertains to the naming and grouping of living organisms. Plants and animals are grouped together by their shared characteristics. The system that is used today includes a family tree-like arrangement that starts out very broadly at the top and becomes narrower and more specific as one goes down each step. At the end is one single animal species.

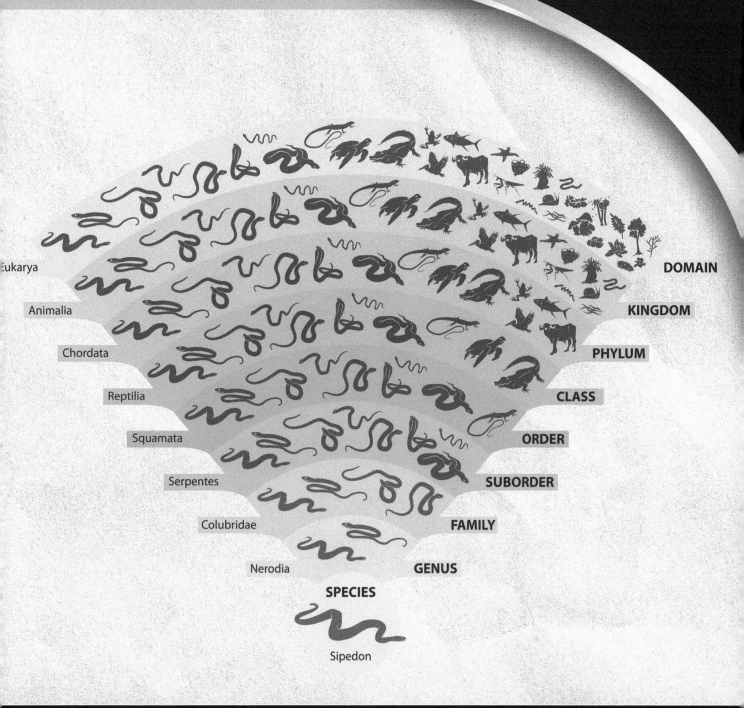

Eukarya — **DOMAIN**

Animalia — **KINGDOM**

Chordata — **PHYLUM**

Reptilia — **CLASS**

Squamata — **ORDER**

Serpentes — **SUBORDER**

Colubridae — **FAMILY**

Nerodia — **GENUS**

SPECIES

Sipedon

THE HIERARCHY OF BIOLOGICAL CLASSIFICATION'S MAJOR
TAXONOMIC RANKS (EXAMPLE OF A SNAKE).

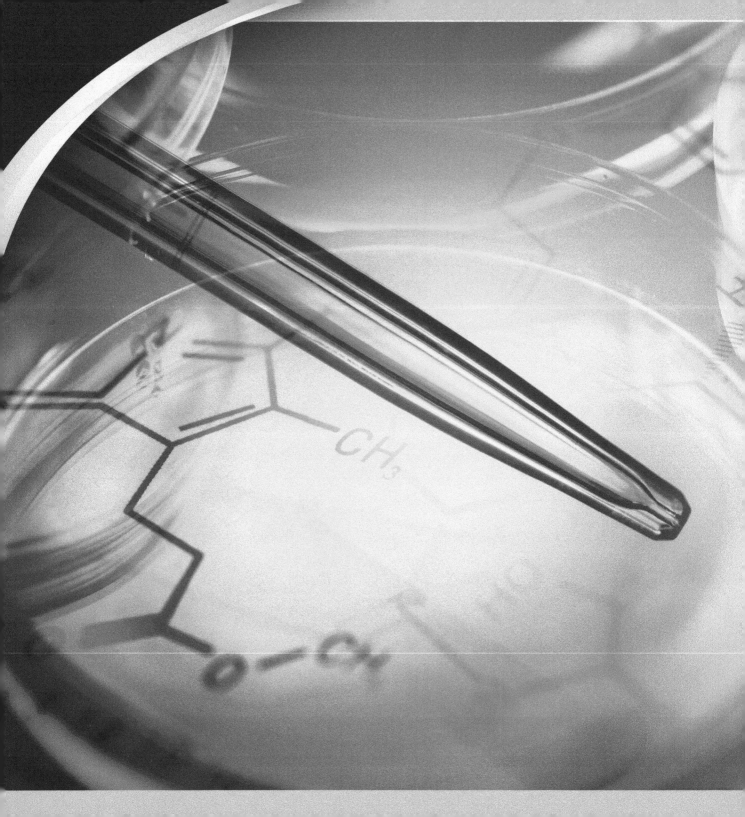

Early Attempts at Classifications

People have tried their hand at classifying living things into an organized system as far back as the ancient Greek philosopher, Aristotle, who lived from 384 to 322 BC.

ARISTOTLE

In his book, *Historia Animalium*, he categorized animals under such headings as "lives on land," "lives on water," "has blood," "does not have blood", and so forth. Aristotle was greatly limited in his efforts to classify all living organisms because he was only aware of the small percentage of plants and animals living in his region.

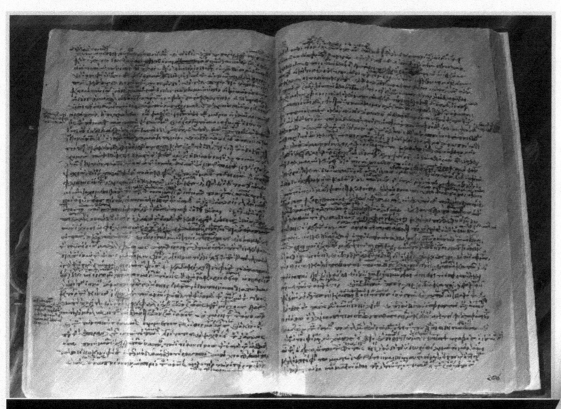

HISTORIA ANIMALIUM IS ONE OF THE MAJOR TEXTS ON BIOLOGY BY THE ANCIENT GREEK PHILOSOPHER ARISTOTLE

He did, however, develop a key aspect of the classification system that proved to be very helpful to Carolus Linnaeus ... the binomial system. "Binomial" means "two names". Aristotle used a "genus", or family name, together with a second name that indicated its difference. This is similar to how many people are named ... with a first name that is individual to you and a last name that indicates your family.

Japanese Maple

Acer
japonica

4

ARISTOTLE USED A "GENUS" TOGETHER WITH A SECOND NAME THAT INDICATED ITS DIFFERENCE.

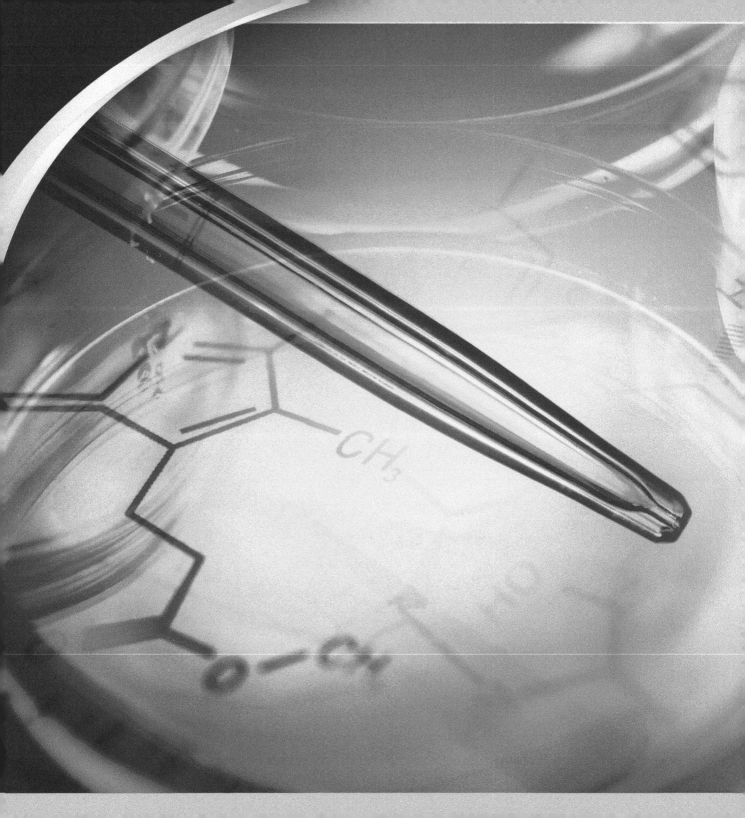

Carolus Linnaeus's Early Years

Carolus Linnaeus considered himself to be a naturalist. Born on May 23, 1707 in Sweden, Linnaeus was so interested in plants that his parents called him "the little botanist" when he was seven or eight years old.

THE FARM AT RASHULT WHERE LINNAEUS WAS BORN.

When he was 20 years old, he enrolled in Uppsala University to study medicine. He paid his tuition by teaching classes in botany. Although he earned his degree in medicine, Linnaeus was more interested in plants than in treating people.

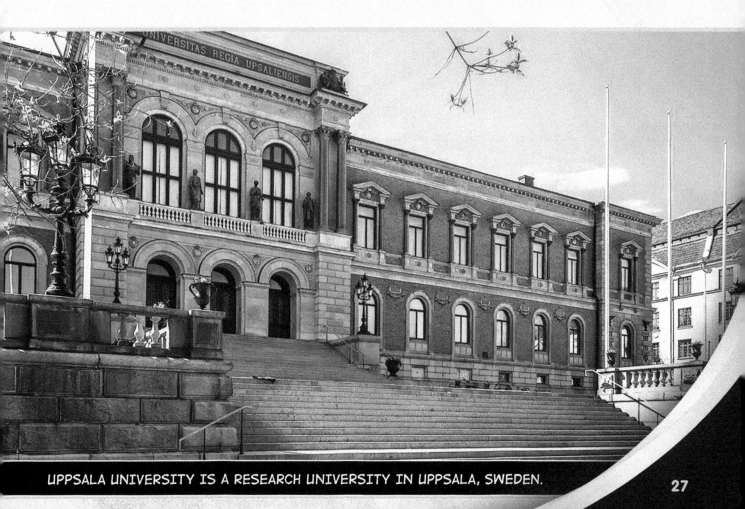

UPPSALA UNIVERSITY IS A RESEARCH UNIVERSITY IN UPPSALA, SWEDEN.

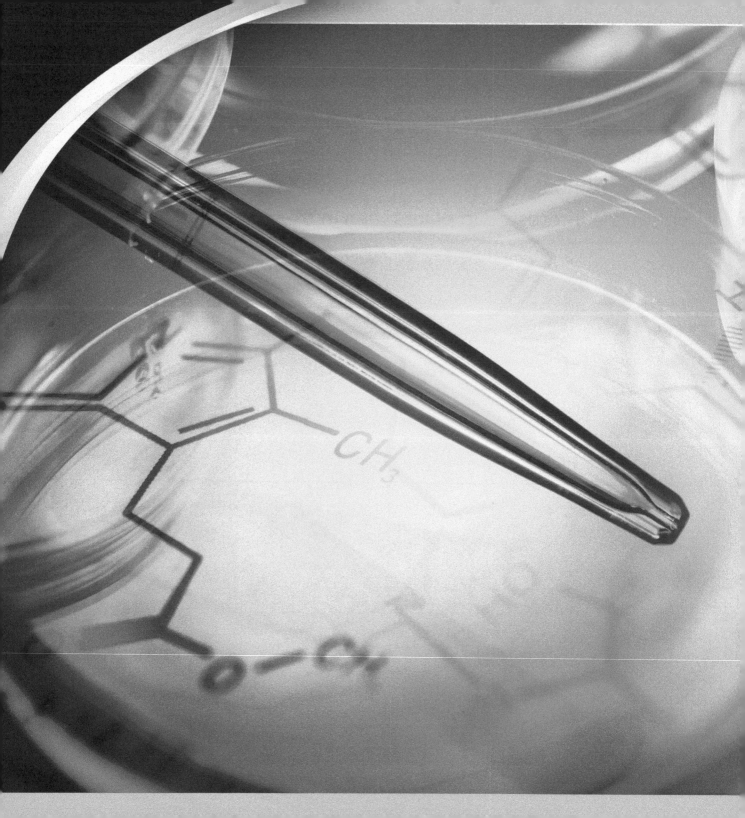

Linnaeus's Big Adventure

While still a student at the university in 1732, Carolus Linnaeus was tapped to embark on a fascinating and dangerous journey. He travelled throughout Lapland, the northernmost part of Europe in present day Finland and Norway, to collect plant specimens and observe the plants of the region.

LINNAEUS IN THE TRADITIONAL DRESS OF THE SAMI PEOPLE OF LAPLAND, HOLDING THE TWINFLOWER THAT BECAME HIS PERSONAL EMBLEM.

LINNAEUS NARROWLY AVOIDING FALLING INTO A CREVASSE WHILST
ON AN EXPEDITION TO LAPLAND, FINLAND IN 1732.

CONTEMPORARY MAP DEPICTING THE SCANDINAVIAN REGION OF EUROPE;
LAPLAND IS THE PALE YELLOW AREA IN THE UPPER-MIDDLE.

Most of Lapland is above the Arctic Circle, yet there is an array of plant life in the region. Linnaeus travelled more than 5,000 miles on this expedition, and, upon his return, he published the notes from his trip in a book called, *Flora Lapponica*.

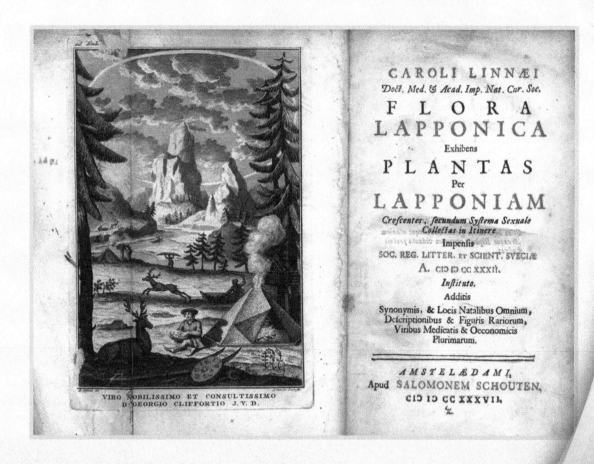

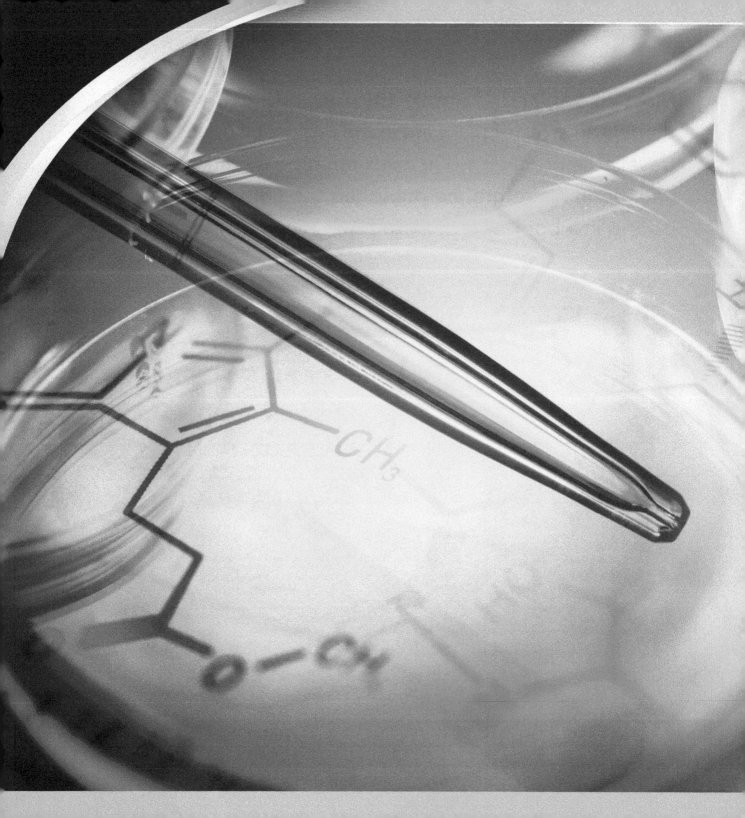

From Med School to a Botanical Garden

After Carolus Linnaeus received his degree in medicine in 1735, he became the director of a prominent botanical garden in Holland. It was there that he devoted much of his time to studying the different plants and recording similarities and differences between them.

LINNAEUS BECAME THE DIRECTOR OF A PROMINENT BOTANICAL GARDEN IN HOLLAND.

He noticed that visiting botanists, from other countries in particular, often referred to plants by different names. This created unneeded confusion. He realized that scientific progress was being stymied by naming issues and set about solving both that problem and the need for a classification system.

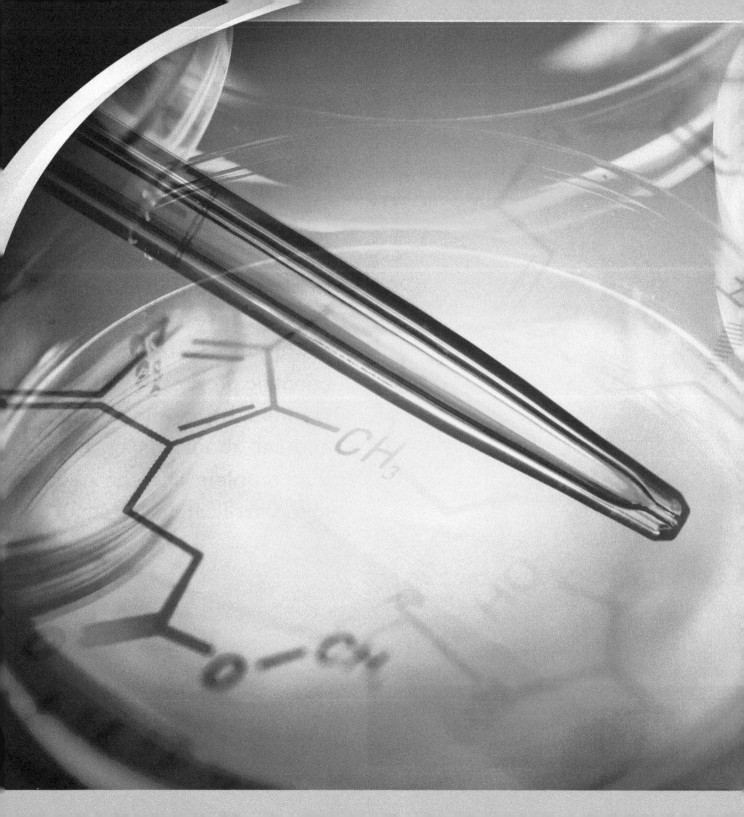

The Father of Taxonomy

Carolus Linnaeus, who lived from 1707 to 1778, has earned the nickname "the Father of Taxonomy." A botanist from Sweden, Linnaeus grew frustrated that there were too many classification systems in use to categorize plants. The systems were inconsistent and fraught with errors. One plant may have numerous scientific names and be classified under more than one heading.

LINNAEUS CLASSIFYING PLANTS IN HIS GARDEN IN SWEDEN.

Linnaeus, who had an interest in botany from an early age, had become a doctor, but still remained interested in plants. Vexed[2] by the inadequate classification systems in use during his time, Linnaeus devoted his energies into developing a viable[3] system.

YOUNG LINNAEUS TIRED OUT AFTER A DAY IN THE FIELDS.

---

2   Vexed – Irritated or annoyed
3   Viable – Workable or capable

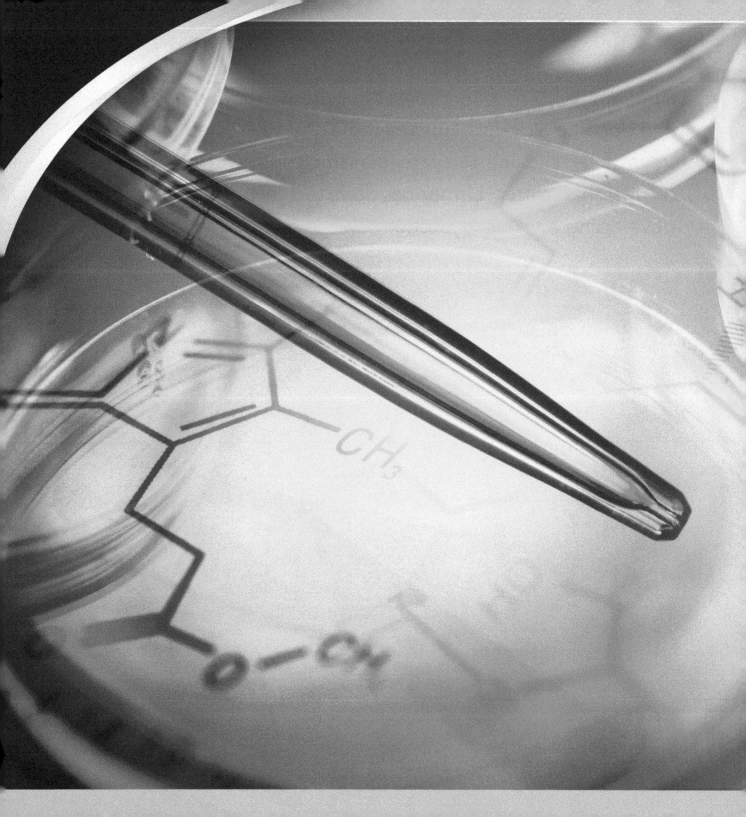

The System
of Nature

In 1735, Carolus Linnaeus published his groundbreaking book, *The System of Nature*. In this book, he set forth his ideas for an all-encompassing and innovative taxonomy system that established a logical framework that is still used today.

CAROLI · LINNÆI, svec

DOCTORIS MEDICINÆ,

SYSTEMA NATURÆ

SIVE

REGNA TRIA NATURÆ

SYSTEMATICE PROPOSITA

PER

CLASSES, ORDINES,
GENERA, & SPECIES.

O JEHOVA! Quam ampla funt opera Tua !
Quam ea omnia fapienter fecifti !
Quam plena eft terra poffeffione tua !
Pfalm. civ. 24.

LUGDUNI BATAVORUM,
Apud THEODORUM HAAK, MDCCX

EX TYPOGRAPHIA
JOANNIS WILHELMI DE GROOT.

In that framework, Linnaeus starts by dividing all living organisms into two categories called kingdoms, one for plants and one for animals. Later, the number of kingdoms was increased to six and now includes fungi and bacteria, among others.

The Six Kingdoms of Life

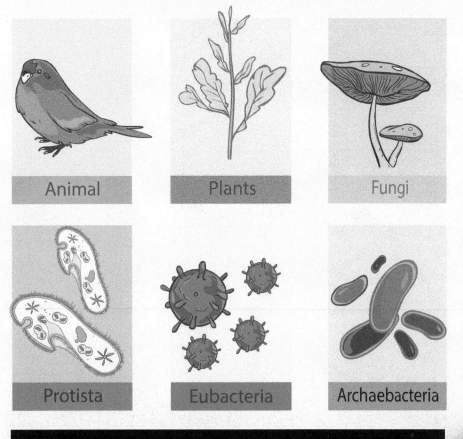

| Animal | Plants | Fungi |
| Protista | Eubacteria | Archaebacteria |

LINNAEUS STARTS BY DIVIDING ALL LIVING
ORGANISMS INTO CATEGORIES CALLED KINGDOMS.

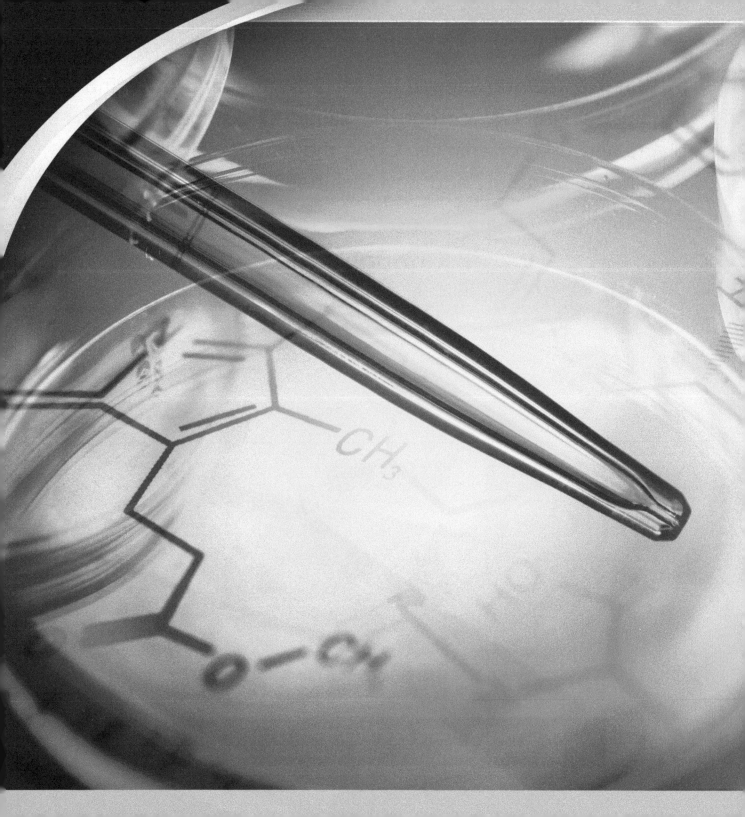

Piggybacking on Aristotle's Work

Carolus Linnaeus borrowed a key concept from Aristotle when he established his taxonomy ... the binomial method. Linnaeus, however, branched out from this starting point to create a *hierarchy*[4] of similar organisms. While Aristotle included the last two levels on the hierarchy – genus and species – Linnaeus added five more steps ... kingdom, phylum, class, order, and family.

---

[4]   Hierarchy – A system of ranking things one above another

CLASSIFICATION SYSTEM

SPECIES

GENUS

FAMILY

ORDER

CLASS

PHYLUM

KINGDOM

VERY
SPECIFIC

VERY
GENERAL

HIERARCHY OF BIOLOGICAL CLASSIFICATION

MOUNTAIN GORILLA

A specific animal may start in the animalia kingdom, then be placed in the phylum for animals with vertebrates[5] and the class of mammals. The class of mammals is broken down into numerous groups. The specific animal in this example will fall under the primate order and the homininae family. Lastly, it belongs to the genus gorilla and the species of beringei … a mountain gorilla.

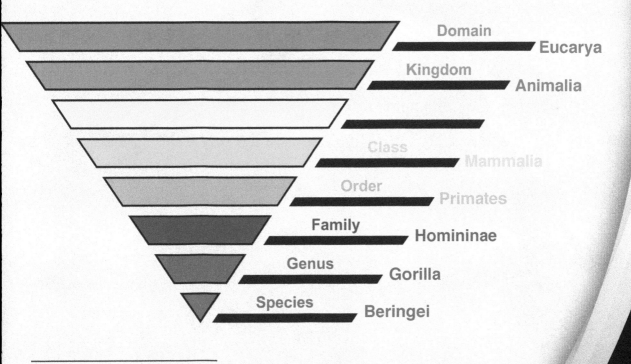

Domain — Eucarya
Kingdom — Animalia
Class — Mammalia
Order — Primates
Family — Homininae
Genus — Gorilla
Species — Beringei

---

5 Vertebrates – Having a backbone

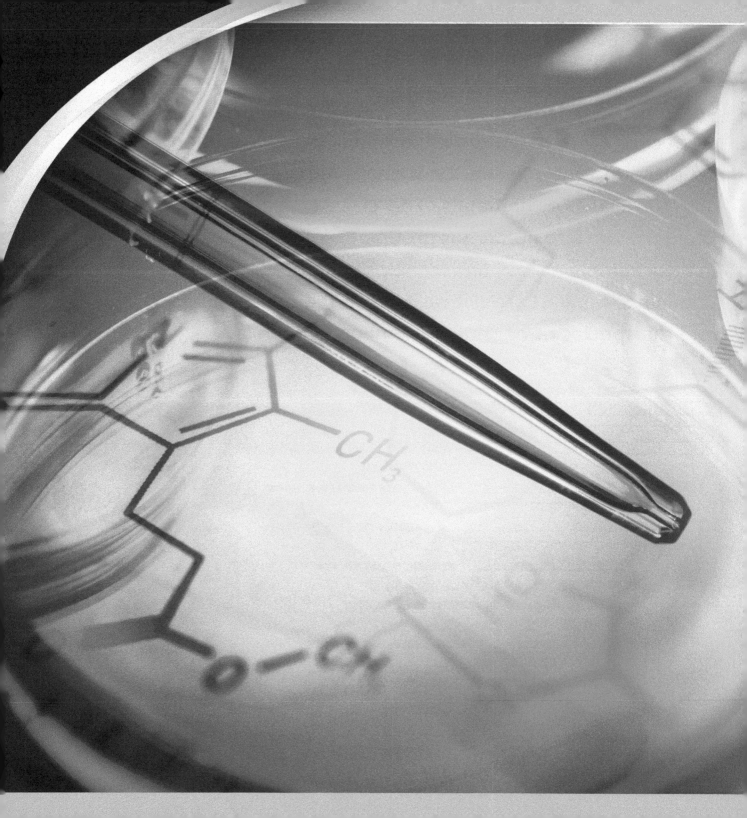

Continuing Work

Linnaeus continued with his work of classifying living organisms and published several updated editions of his The System of Nature, as well as a book devoted entirely to the classification of plants, The Species of Plants.

CAROLI LINNÆI

Equitis aur. de Stella polari,

ARCHIATRI REGII, MED. & BOTAN. PROFESS. UPSAL.
ACAD. UPSAL. HOLMENS. PETROPOL. BEROL. IMPERIAL.
LONDIN. MONSPEL. TOLOS. FLORENT. SOC.

SPECIES PLANTARUM,

EXHIBENTES
PLANTAS RITE COGNITAS,
AD
GENERA RELATAS,
CUM
DIFFERENTIIS SPECIFICIS,
NOMINIBUS TRIVIALIBUS,
SYNONYMIS SELECTIS,
LOCIS NATALIBUS,
SECUNDUM
SYSTEMA SEXUALE
DIGESTAS.

TOMUS I.

Editio Secunda, aucta.

Cum Privilegio S. R. M:tis Sveciæ & S. R. M:tis Poloniæ ac Electoris Saxon.

HOLMIÆ
IMPENSIS DIRECT. LAURENTII SALVII
1762.

TITLE PAGE OF 'SPECIES PLANTARUM',
BY CAROLUS LINNAEUS, 1762.

CARL VON LINNE

LINNAEUS WAS A GREAT CLASSIFIER
OF LIVING ORGANISMS.

Over the course of his academic work, Carolus Linnaeus amassed[6] a collection of plants and animals that numbered more than 40,000 specimens. From studying these specimens, he was able to classify and scientifically name more than 4,400 species of animals and nearly 8,000 species of plants.

---

[6] Amassed – Collected or gathered together

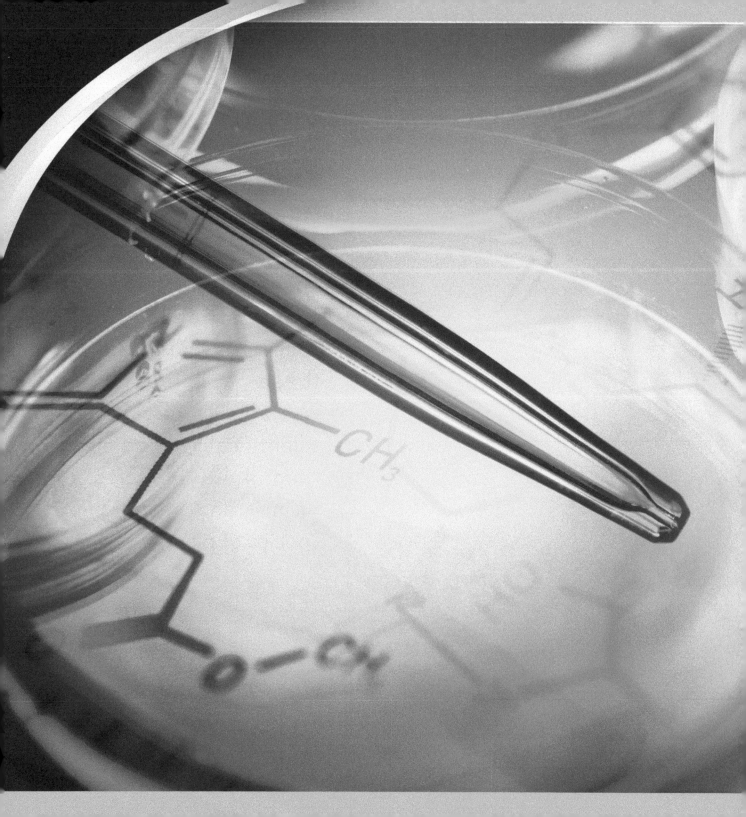

Linnaeus and Latin

One of the sources of confusion in the earlier classification systems was the language. When scientists name plants and animals using words from their own native tongue, it leaves room for error and misinterpretations. To solve this problem, Carolus Linnaeus, and other scientists, began to use Latin as a common language of science. The reasons for choosing Latin were twofold.

LINNAEUS AND OTHER SCIENTISTS BEGAN TO USE LATIN AS A COMMON LANGUAGE OF SCIENCE.

First, since no one speaks Latin anymore, it makes it a neutral language. If a living language, like French or English, was picked to be the official language of science, some countries may feel it gives an unfair advantage to some scientists over others. Second, Latin is a dead language. That means it is not changing and evolving like other languages. The words that were assigned to species two centuries ago still mean the same thing because the language isn't being influenced by its speakers. Linnaeus was such a fan of Latin that he even changed his first name, Carl, to the Latin version, Carolus.

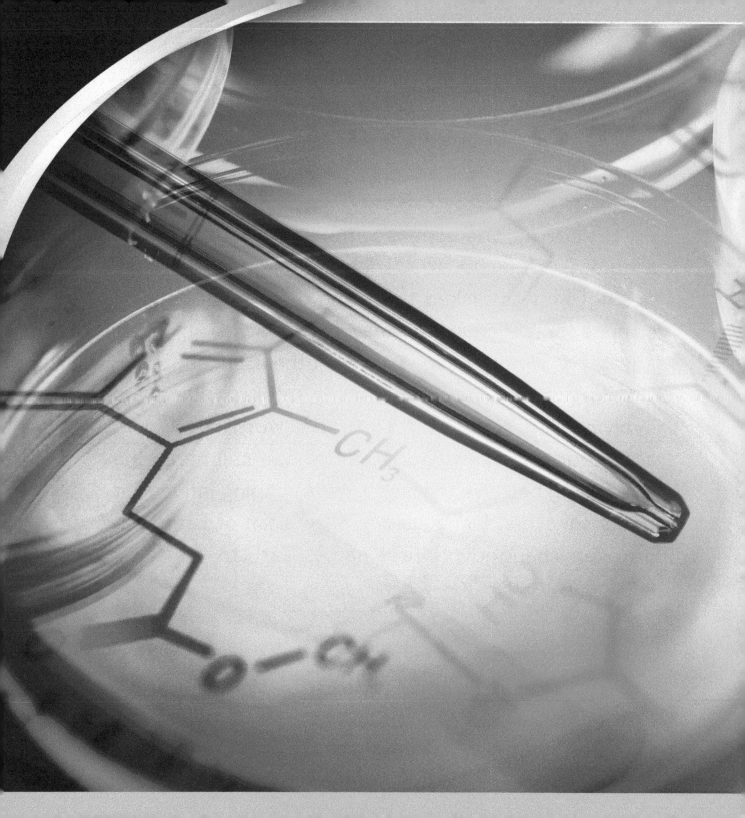

Mystical Additions to Linnaeus's Taxonomy

Many of the plants and animals included in *The System of Nature*, by Carolus Linnaeus, were living things that Linnaeus had not witnessed for himself. Instead, the information about them was given to him by outside sources – sailors or explorers who claimed to have seen them or written accounts in ancient texts. Because of this, Linnaeus included taxonomies for imaginary mythical creatures, including the unicorn, hydra, phoenix, and satyr. These entries are often referred to as *Animalia Paradoxa*, or "contradictory animals". In the 6th edition of *The System of Nature*, which was released in 1748, the *Animalia Paradoxa*[7] were removed.

---

[7] Paradox – Contradictory or false

UNICORN

HYDRA

PHOENIX

SATYR

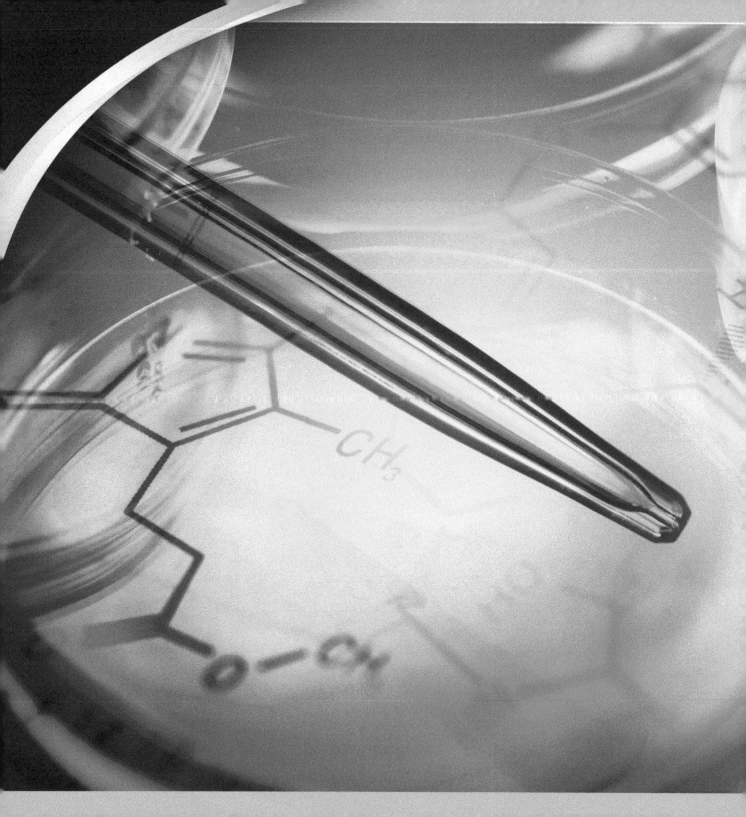

Adopting Linnaeus's Taxonomy

It was a huge and daunting task, but Carolus Linnaeus was able to develop a taxonomy system that was thorough, all-encompassing, logical, and left very little room for error. His work was far superior to other, earlier attempts at classification systems, therefore his system was widely adopted by scientists.

LINNAEUS WAS ABLE TO DEVELOP A TAXONOMY SYSTEM THAT WAS THOROUGH, ALL-ENCOMPASSING, LOGICAL, AND LEFT VERY LITTLE ROOM FOR ERROR.

Like all good scientific systems, Linnaeus's taxonomy has been able to stand the test of time because it is flexible and adaptable. It has been tweaked over the years, with changes and additions to reflect new scientific knowledge and discoveries. Overall, the taxonomy has been successful at its intended purpose ... to give biologists the data they need to compare similar and dissimilar living organisms.

TAXONOMY GIVES BIOLOGISTS THE DATA THEY NEED TO COMPARE SIMILAR AND DISSIMILAR LIVING ORGANISMS.

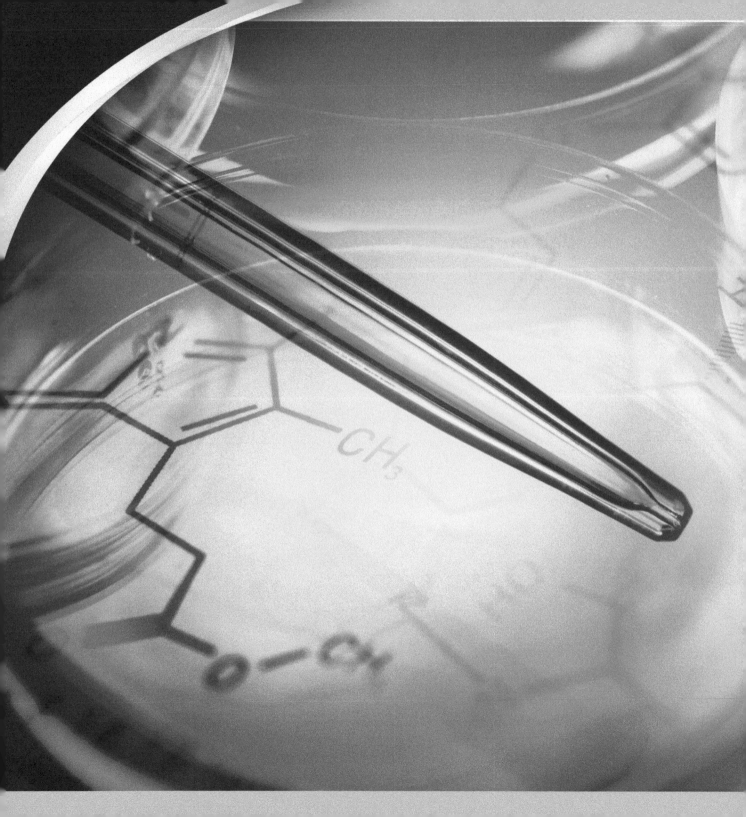

Summary

A Swedish botanist named Carolus Linnaeus devoted his life to the naming and classification of plants and animals into a taxonomy that he created. His system was logical, thorough, and designed to eliminate confusion. His system was composed of seven layers or tiers – kingdom, phylum, class, order, family, genus, and species – that started at the broadest description and became more and more focused on each tier until only one animal remained. His system was so effective that scientists are still using it today.

STATUE OF CAROLUS LINNAEUS, AT THE CHICAGO BOTANIC GARDENS, GLENCOE, ILLINOIS

Now that you know about the significant work of Carolus Linnaeus, you should look at the important contributions made by other early naturalists.

Lightning Source UK Ltd.
Milton Keynes UK
UKHW051701060121
376449UK00004B/64

9 781541 979543